Original title:
Sleigh Bells in the Snow

Copyright © 2024 Creative Arts Management OÜ
All rights reserved.

Author: Simon Fairchild
ISBN HARDBACK: 978-9916-90-892-1
ISBN PAPERBACK: 978-9916-90-893-8

Dance of the Frozen Echoes

Frosty air and giggles rise,
Snowmen wobble with silly eyes.
Gloves too big and noses bright,
We'll dance around until the night.

Jingle hats upon our heads,
Chasing snowflakes, no time for beds.
Socks are soggy, hats are askew,
Creating chaos, with laughter too!

Harmonies Beneath the Winter Sky

Boots that slip on icy trails,
Singing loudly, off-key wails.
Giggling friends in frozen cheer,
Jumpsuits help us hug the beer.

Chill winds toss our playful hair,
We chase the snow, we just don't care.
Frosty breath and rosy cheeks,
Winter's full of fun-filled peaks.

Cherished Moments in Icy Stillness

Snowflakes fall like silly dreams,
Hot cocoa slips and steamy beams.
Snowball fights and squealed delight,
Who knew winter could be so bright?

Skates that wobble on the pond,
Falling down, we laugh, we're fond.
With every slip and icy twist,
We find the joy that can't be missed.

A Tapestry of Snow and Sound

Snowmen ring with hats askew,
While puppies bounce like they're brand new.
A snowstorm's tug on our wild play,
Frosted fun will rule the day!

Snowflakes sprinkle like confetti,
And in this cold, we feel all warm and petty.
In a flurry of laughter and joyful shouts,
We freeze this moment, without doubts.

Glimmering Tracks in the Twilight

Through the twinkling sparkle, we skate,
Laughter dangles on each cold plate.
A whoops and a slip, oh what a sight,
As snowflakes dance in the fading light.

With candy canes held high in cheer,
We glide and giggle, no hint of fear.
Frosty whiskers on every face,
Each tumble shows our charming grace.

Magic of a Winter Soundscape

The air is filled with hoots and yells,
As we whizz down hills with icy swells.
A plop and a splash, giggles abound,
In winter's grip, joy is unbound.

Hot cocoa dribbles, marshmallow fights,
Chasing each other in fanciful flights.
Snowmen wiggle with carrot noses,
And we burrow deep in fluffy roses.

Moonlit Trails of Laughter

Under the stars, we waddle like ducks,
With frosty breath, we share our luck.
A tumble, a roll, on a snowy hill,
Hearts race high as we catch the thrill.

Snowballs flying, laughter so bright,
We're merry mischief-makers all night.
In this winter wonder, all worries flee,
As giggles wrap 'round like cozy tea.

Frosty Footprints and Echoed Songs

Across the white, our footprints trace,
Jumping high, we challenge space.
With each silly dance and twirl,
Winter whispers, bright and twirled.

A chorus of chuckles fills the air,
Making snow angels without a care.
The chill can't freeze our merry spree,
As we jingle joyfully, wild and free.

The Symphony of Frosty Nights

In winter's grip, we start to slide,
With laughter loud and glee as our guide.
Snowflakes fall like gentle pranks,
We glide on ice, our pants in janks.

Hot cocoa spills, a sweet delight,
We tumble down in frosty night.
Winter's tune is quite the show,
With slips and trips as we all go.

Chilled Glances and Rushing Breezes

Through swirling winds, we giggle and shout,
'Tis not my hat, it's a snowman, no doubt!
Eyes wide open and cheeks all aglow,
We race on snow, not sure where to go.

A snowball flies, it makes a whack,
And from my friend, I hear a 'crack!'
We roll in piles, making snow foes,
In this chilly chaos, friendship grows.

Starlit Stories of Mirth

Under stars that twinkle so bright,
We gather 'round, what a silly sight!
Tales of giants and penguins, oh dear,
As snowflakes dance and winter draws near.

Mittens mismatched, we laugh in delight,
While ducks in scarves take flight, what a sight!
In the frosty air, our laughter rings,
With shovels and shenanigans, who needs kings?

Rhythms in the Winter's Hold

The world outside plays a chilly beat,
With snowy steps, we shuffle our feet.
A joyous jig on crisp white ground,
Where giggles and gasps are the only sound.

So let us dance with snowflakes fair,
And make snow angels in frosty air.
With every slip, our hearts take flight,
In this funny season, all feels just right.

Winter's Whispering Jingle

In winter's chill, joy takes its flight,
A cat in boots, what a silly sight!
Snowmen dance, in attire so bright,
They wobble and giggle, a comical fright.

Hot cocoa spills, with marshmallows afloat,
A penguin slides down, on a slippery boat.
The taste of laughter, we lovingly gloat,
While reindeer prance, in a mismatched coat.

Chimes of Frosted Dreams

A squirrel in socks, what a sight to behold,
Stealing my snack, with a heart full of bold.
The snowflakes giggle as they twirl and fold,
While snowmen argue, their noses turn gold.

A penguin's parade, in the middle of June,
Shuffling and dancing, making quite a tune.
The moonlight sparkles, as bright as a balloon,
In this frosty chaos, we all hum a tune.

Echoes Through the Silent Woods

Snow crunches under, tiny paws scamper,
A bear in slippers steals my hot champer.
While owls exchange jokes, they're quite the pamper,
As trees whisper secrets, their roots entwine, camper.

A snowball fight, oh what a grand mess,
With laughter and giggles, who needs to impress?
Bunnies in bows, causing sheer distress,
As winter's delight turns playful, no less.

Frosty Lullabies Under Moonlight

Chattering critters, in frosty delight,
A raccoon in pajamas, oh what a sight!
Huddled together, their jokes take to flight,
While stars twinkle down, in the cold of the night.

The moon grins wide, with a silvery gleam,
As children play dress-up, in a dreamlike theme.
Frosty-skinned people, giggling in streams,
In snow-covered lands, we all share our dreams.

Chimes of the Chilled Night

In winter coats, we huddle tight,
With candy canes, we start our flight.
The frosty air ignites our cheer,
As laughter dances, drawing near.

The snowmen's hats are far too low,
They wobble as they say hello.
With giggles echoing through the park,
We trip and slide, laugh till it's dark.

The Sound of Joy on Ice

With tiny skates, we glide and sway,
But then I trip, and yell, "Hooray!"
I land on ice, a comical sight,
As friends all gather, sharing delight.

The penguins dance, or so I claim,
While I create my own new game.
Falling down is quite the show,
The chuckles grow with every throw.

Laughter Amidst the Snowflakes

The flakes come down, a fluffy storm,
We build a fort, bizarrely warm.
Snowballs flying, dodge and weave,
In this mad winter, we believe.

With scarves tied tight, we make our stand,
A snowball fight, oh, wasn't that grand?
Each toss and shout, a raucous sound,
In this winter's joy, we're truly found.

Frost-kissed Melodies

The hot cocoa spills, oh what a mess,
With whipped cream hats, a frosty dress.
We laugh aloud and sip too fast,
Each chilly sip, a joyful blast.

As icicles hang and sparkle bright,
We dance around till late at night.
With frosted voices, we sing and rhyme,
In this silly world, we're lost in time.

Delights on Drifting Snowdrifts

Snowflakes tumble, twist and glide,
Hot cocoa waits, a drink inside.
But here I sink, up to my waist,
My scarf has made a snowy paste!

As snowmen form with crooked grins,
They'll never win the warm-up wins.
I build a fort, it's quite the scene,
But someone starts a snowball spree!

Nightfall's Quiet Revelry in White

The moonlight gleams on icy ground,
While cats in boots are prowling 'round.
Mice in mittens run for their cheese,
Each thump, a festive tale to tease!

A family tumbles, giggle and roll,
While dad recounts his icy stroll.
Oh, watch him slip, a sight to see,
The starry night gives joy and glee!

Celestial Sounds on a Starry Night

Stars are laughing, can't you hear?
A carol sung by frosty cheer.
Trees wear coats of glimmering light,
And squirrels dance with pure delight.

The hot pie's stolen by a sneaky crow,
He flies off quick, it's quite the show!
While snowflakes whirl in frosty grace,
The laughter bounces, fills the space.

Carols of the Glittering Aglow

Glistening night has sparks of fun,
Pinecones pelt my brother's run.
Mom finds joy in tiny pranks,
With tangled lights that fill the ranks.

But chilly winds bring silly hats,
As snowflakes fall on fluffy cats.
The merry sights bring laughter's glow,
In frosty air, we play in tow.

A Journey Through the Gleaming Silence

Beneath the twinkling stars so bright,
We careen in circles, what a sight!
Laughing snowmen fall with a thud,
As we glide past a frosty mud.

Hot cocoa spills in a throwing spree,
While everyone wears their slippers with glee.
The snowflakes dance, a surprising cheer,
As we hop and tumble, a little unclear.

Glistening paths lead us to a feast,
Where cookies and jokes are shared, at least.
A snowball fight breaks out with a grin,
And someone ducks—then lands in the bin!

So here we go with laughter in tow,
In this trip of giggles, we paint the snow.
The night's filled with joy, with friends all around,
In this white wonderland, silliness abound.

Sprites of Frost and Joyful Laughter.

Chilly breezes play a merry tune,
As we sail past in a jolly balloon.
The snowmen wave, looking quite round,
We trip and stumble, face first in the ground.

With muffled giggles, we pop and spin,
Donning our hats, tucked under chin.
A snowflake lands right on my nose,
Then off it slips, as laughter grows.

Elves in the forest giggle and prance,
They yell, "Join us!" and boot us to dance.
We leap and twirl, all arms and legs,
Somewhere a snowplow chokes on its eggs.

The stars twinkle bright on this chilly night,
Our frosty faces beam with delight.
In this playful world, there's cheer without end,
Joyful spirits abound, with laughter to send.

Winter Whispers in Frost

The air is crisp, so jokes are told,
As chilly ghosts form shapes so bold.
We chuckle along the snowy lane,
Where giggling gnomes dance in the rain.

A tumble here and a slip over there,
With cheeks aglow, with style and flair.
Snowflakes stick to our marshmallow hats,
As we race by with friendly spats.

Snow angels flap their wings so wide,
As we try hard not to turn and glide.
A friendly bear rolls by with a grin,
With our tangled shouts, the fun can begin!

So let's chase the moon with a hearty cheer,
In this frosty realm, there's nothing to fear.
With laughter echoing beneath the night,
Winter's humor makes everything bright.

Echoes of a Frosty Evening

Under the moonlight, we boldly tread,
With scarves that dance, and hats that spread.
A mischievous fox winks at our play,
As we stumble along, giggling away.

A toss of snowballs turns into a scheme,
While our cheeks match the blush of a dream.
Bouncing off trees like ping pong balls,
Our laughter echoes as the evening calls.

Snowflakes pirouette, a whimsical sight,
While friends trip over their wishes tonight.
We spin in circles, till we feel quite dizzy,
Making this winter ever so fizzy.

With pinky promises, we bask in delight,
On this precious journey, all through the night.
Laughter lingers in the icy air,
As we celebrate winter's playful flair.

A Winter's Serenade to Remember

In a blanket of white, we twirl with glee,
Making snow angels as happy as can be.
Frosty mustaches on snowmen we make,
Waving at reindeer who start to awake.

Hot cocoa spills on our mittens so bright,
While penguin slides turn our laughter to flight.
Oh, what a scene, with our cheeks all aglow,
Who knew winter could be such a show?

We race on our sleds, and we tumble and fall,
Emerging all giggles when we hear the call.
"Let's build an igloo!" our buddy then cries,
But it ends up a snow fort where snowballs fly!

As night settles in, snowflakes start to glow,
We promise this moment we'll never outgrow.
With snowflakes like sprinkles and stars up above,
Winter's a frolic, oh joy, oh love!

Cold Magic and Warm Hearts

With nippy toes tapping on icy old ground,
We dance in the streets, laughter's echoing sound.
The dog in a sweater, so dapper and proud,
He prances around, drawing quite a crowd.

Hot apple cider, a warm sugary treat,
We giggle and chatter, it can't be beat!
Snowflakes tumble down, oh what a delight,
Each flake holding secrets that shimmer in light.

A snowball flies by, it gleefully whizzes,
Dodging the laughter, oh, how the storm sizzles!
With snowmen so silly, each one has a grin,
Who knew Mr. Frosty had humor within?

Under twinkling lights, we sing with pure cheer,
Winter's fun magic brings everyone near.
A jolly endeavor, warm hearts all aglow,
With snow kicking up joy, we steal the show!

Snowy Night Tales of Bliss

A yarn about snowflakes with quirks and a twist,
One claimed to be shy while another got kissed.
They hop from the clouds, taking turns in their flight,
Leaving behind stories that sparkle at night.

The rabbit who slides right out of view,
Lands in a snowbank and says, "How do you do?"
He giggles and hops, as we all watch the fun,
Whispering secrets till the day is done.

The stars gather round, twinkling jests overhead,
While snowmen engage in a hilarious spread.
They tell silly jokes that would make you split,
With punchlines that come from each frosty wit.

As we settle in, cozy blankets in tow,
The stories grow richer, the laughter will flow.
Oh, wintery nights filled with fanciful dreams,
Embracing the magic in all its bright beams!

Murmurs of a Frosty Eve

Frosty critters prance about,
Slipping, sliding, full of doubt.
Snowflakes laugh as they go by,
Hats fly off, oh what a lie!

Chubby cheeks in puffer coats,
Zooming down on makeshift boats.
Hot cocoa spills, a big oops here,
Giggling bright, we'll persevere!

Frosted noses, cheeks like blooms,
Snowman's hat got stuck in rooms.
Found him grinning, arms out wide,
Did I say he's my snow-slide?

Snowball fights and laughter loud,
Wrapping up inside the crowd.
Frosty fun that makes us cheer,
Winter's jokes, we hold so dear.

Glacial Serenades at Dusk

Ducks in scarves on frozen lakes,
Waddling round, what funny shakes!
Ice creams made of snowy fluff,
Are we sure this isn't tough?

Snowmen strut with carrot grins,
Swinging arms and silly spins.
Each snowflake winks, a funny sight,
Cackling during winter's night.

Socks on hands, oh what a sight,
Chasing shadows with delight.
Laughter echoes through the chill,
What is this? A snowball thrill?

Under stars that twinkle bright,
We dare to dance in pure delight.
Frosty friends, a party true,
Jokes on ice are all we do!

Joy in the Heart of Winter

Toboggan rides at breakneck speed,
Who knew snow could make a need?
Wipeouts happen, laughter flows,
Each tumbling fall, oh how it grows!

In a flurry, snowflakes fight,
Dancing round, our pure delight.
Snowy beards on faces swell,
Telling tales of winter's spell.

Carrots fetch the snowman's nose,
Most of them, he simply throws.
Giggles stuck in frozen breath,
Jokes abound until our death!

Hot spuds roast, oh what a feast,
Winter's joy is nothing least.
In this chill, where hearts collide,
Laughter makes the snow abide.

Melodies from a Snowy Hearth

Warm blankets piled, we sit tight,
Crackling fire, oh what a sight!
Snow drifts dance outside the door,
All the while, we laugh and snore.

On a whim, we start to sing,
Out of tune, it's such a fling!
Snowmen listen, with delight,
They're our band, all through the night.

Cookies baked, now crumbs do fly,
Gingerbread folks fight on the sly.
Frosty mouths echo with glee,
Tell your friends, come join our spree!

Mugs of cheer and tasty treats,
Winter joy, in quirky beats.
As the world wraps up in white,
Laughter warms this chilly night.

The Enchanted Icebound Ballad

In winter's grasp, the snowflakes twirl,
The penguin's dance makes me want to hurl.
A squirrel chased a snowman once,
But slipped on ice; oh what a dunce!

His hat flew off, like a kite in flight,
The night was cold, but the laughter's bright.
We built a fort with a questionable aim,
And lost a snowball fight; what a shame!

The snowplow roars, it's quite the sight,
I dodged a flake, then slipped in fright.
The dog thinks it's a game to chase,
But all he finds is white, cold space!

A cup of cocoa spills on my lap,
While we huddle tight in the winter's trap.
So raise your mugs to this frosty fun,
And let the games begin, everyone!

Winter's Lullaby in the Stillness

The snowflakes fall, soft and slow,
A rabbit slips on ice below.
In knitted sweaters, kids do play,
While grandma warns, 'Stay out of sway!'

Laughter echoes through the air,
As snowballs fly without a care.
Hot cocoa spills across my hand,
I'm afraid of falling in this land!

The frost has turned my hair to white,
I'm sorry penguins, it's not polite.
They waddle past with much delight,
As snowmen melt by morning light.

With gumdrops stuck on every tree,
Oh look, a deer has come to see!
We share a laugh with nature's cheer,
While winter's warmth brings us near!

Rhapsody of the Wintry Wilderness

In drifts of white, they dance and twirl,
The snowflakes spin, the wild winds whirl.
A hedgehog dons a tiny hat,
While rabbits plot their sneaky spat.

The skis go flying, oh what a fate,
As friends collide, they hastily skate.
We laugh until our cheeks turn red,
I think I've tangled in the sled!

A igloo formed, a brief affair,
Our snowman's nose is a juicy pear!
We race again, the finish near,
But someone tumbled, laughing fierce!

So gather round, we'll sing a tune,
An ode to winter and silly shoon.
Our playful hearts will always glow,
As laughter fills this frosty show!

The Glint of Joy in the Pale Moonlight

The moon shines bright on frozen ground,
A snowflake lands; it makes no sound.
But look! A cat's in quite a fix,
She wrapped her tail in snowy tricks!

The owls hoot, a quirky choir,
As kids set off their small, loud pyre.
With flaming marshmallows on a stick,
We roast and joke, a tasty trick!

The snowman's head took off in glee,
With a carrot nose, he danced with me.
And when it melts, we cheer and clap,
This wacky winter's nonsensical rap!

Ice-skates clatter against the song,
As ice-thrones crown where we belong.
We hoot and holler, the night is gay,
In moonlit fun, we laugh away!

Starlit Frost and Joyful Echoes

Under twinkling stars so bright,
We skate and tumble, what a sight!
Our snacks are slipping, hot cocoa spills,
Laughter echoes through the hills.

In the chilly air, we sing,
With rhymes and giggles, joy they bring.
Chasing snowflakes, we play like kids,
Knocking over large snowdrift lids.

As we wipe the snow from our cheeks,
Someone's sleds are lost for weeks!
Rolling down hills, they trip and fall,
But oh, how we adore it all!

Frosty air can't freeze our cheer,
We spin and dance, no rush or fear.
With each playful, icy prank,
We fill our hearts, a joyous bank.

Tinkling Tunes in the Frozen Air

Snowflakes whisper on the breeze,
We hear them giggle through the trees.
Mittens on and scarves so bright,
We prance around, what pure delight!

A snowman stands, quite round and fat,
Wearing a wig—yes, he's a brat!
We toss him snowballs, he won't mind,
He's chilled out and so refined.

With hot cocoa, fingers numb,
We cheer our friends, come one, come some!
Catching snowballs, dodging fast,
With frosty fun that's sure to last.

Our laughter's loud as we parade,
Around the trees, a jolly brigade.
In this winter wonderland fair,
We frolic and sing, without a care.

A Festival of Frosty Melodies

A frosty morn, we take our cue,
With sleds in tow, we'll slide on through.
Our hats are tipped, our cheeks are red,
Dodging snowballs atop our sled!

In the air, there's music sweet,
A band of squirrels with dancing feet.
Down the slope, a crash and boom,
Out from the woods, comes laughter's zoom!

Snowmen waltz in their frosty style,
Winking at us with a snowy smile.
We join the dance, it's quite the show,
With jigs and twists, we steal the snow!

At the end of day, we gather near,
With tales of fun and festive cheer.
In this winter carnival bright,
We'll hold these moments, pure delight.

Frosty Walking in Wonderland

Frosty feet in a world of white,
We slip and slide, oh what a sight!
Snowflakes fall like wishes made,
We watch our footprints, a lovely parade.

With pockets full of secrets sweet,
We dash and dart down every street.
Chasing each other, bright and bold,
In this playground where dreams unfold.

Snowball fights and playful screams,
Rolling in snow, lost in our dreams.
The moon is rising, the night is young,
Let's sing to the stars, our hearts are strung!

With chilly cheeks and joyful hearts,
We know this fun will never part.
A winter tale that feels so right,
In frosty wonderland of night.

Echoing Footsteps on Icy Paths

Crunching sounds beneath my feet,
I glide and slip, my swift retreat.
A tumble here, a giggle there,
And winter's laughter fills the air.

Snowflakes wink from branches high,
As I attempt to leap and fly.
A snowball fight, oh what a blast,
I throw it well, but slip at last.

Twirling round, I spinning dance,
While snowmen look, without a chance.
With carrot noses on their face,
I land in snow, an icy grace.

The cold might bite, but so what, hey?
I'll chase the chill with playful sway.
Through frozen paths, I skip with glee,
As winter frolics, wild and free.

Rhythms of Frost on Ebon Canvas

The world is white, a canvas vast,
My boots arrive, they stomp and blast.
A high heel slip, a woeful sound,
As I flail around, it's frosty ground.

The laughter flows, a jingling tune,
As snowmen sway beneath the moon.
They nod their heads, they think it sly,
As I go woosh, then why oh why?

A snowbank beckons, oh so grand,
I leap inside, it's not well planned.
I pop back up, my cheeks so red,
I see the dog, and he's full sped!

Paw prints dance where I fell flat,
In winter's joke, we all can chat.
So here we go, let's step and spin,
In this white wonder, let fun begin!

Bursts of Joy Amidst the White

With arms flailing, I start to play,
In fluffy mounds of white array.
Snowballs flying, and laughter loud,
While icy trolls, I've lost the crowd.

The frosty air is crisp and pure,
As well-placed snowballs make me sure.
Each burst of joy is filled with snow,
But watch out now, or you might go!

My scarf does twist just like my fate,
As I slip sideways, it's pretty great.
Snowflakes tickle as they spin and whirl,
With mittened hands, I give a twirl.

We skate and slide, hearts full of cheer,
With every slip, we draw near.
So let's proclaim, in frosty jest,
Winter's wonder is truly the best!

The Soft Serenade of Winter's Embrace

Beneath a sky of twinkling stars,
I'm not alone, I've got my scars.
Each step I take is filled with flair,
For every tumble, there's snow to share.

The moonlight glimmers on the street,
As icy breezes sound so sweet.
With every step, my laughter peals,
I slide like penguins on their heels.

Snowflakes whirl with a gossiping sound,
As friends all gather, laughing around.
In the chill, our spirits rise,
With every slip, a new surprise.

The night rolls on with joy and cheer,
As winter sings, we have no fear.
So here's to fun, to frosty doses,
In every flake, the laughter roses.

Whispers of a Wintry Wind

The wind was a rascal, blowing so free,
Knocked my hat off, oh dear me!
Chasing it down the frosty lane,
With every slip, I'd dance and feign.

Snowflakes were plotting a slippery fate,
Twirling like dancers, oh how they skate!
I tripped in a pile, face-first in the fluff,
The laughter erupted, it sure was tough!

My scarf took a tumble, on a branch it did cling,
Like a cheery old flag, it made the birds sing.
I waved it around, with a goofy grin wide,
Wishing for cocoa, right by my side!

But oh, what a sight, my snowman of cheer,
With a wonky carrot, it brought such good cheer!
It waved to the kids as they skied down the way,
Who knew frosty fun could brighten the day?

Jingle Rhythms in the Cold

In the brisk chill, I frolic and play,
My boots squeak loudly, come join the ballet!
Snowmen in top hats just can't hold it together,
When I take a tumble, it's glorious weather!

With mittens so bright, I fly through the flakes,
Each snowball I toss, oh boy, what mistakes!
But laughter erupts when my aim goes askew,
Snow-covered giggles, the best kind of glue.

Hot chocolate beckons from the snug hearth inside,
As I prance like a penguin, with arms open wide.
My friends call me silly, but I just can't stop,
Rolling and tumbling, right down to the shop!

Jingly treats dangling from my coat and my cap,
A sleigh ride on laughter, nestled snug in a nap.
When winter unwinds, my heart starts to race,
Just a silly little snowflake, finding its place!

Holiday Harmony Under a Blanket of White

Beneath the white sheets, a chorus unfolds,
I waltz through the snow as the evening grows cold.
Each step a giggle, each slip a surprise,
Who knew winter could bring such wild eyes?

Snowballs are flying, my friends in delight,
The snowman's got style, it's quite the sight!
A carrot nose crooked, like a joke gone awry,
With arms made of branches, he winks at the sky!

We gather for cocoa, it warms all our hearts,
While discussing the merits of snowballing arts.
One tiny mishap leads to howling loud mirth,
As we tumble and roll in the soft, snowy earth.

So here's to the joy that the chill does bestow,
With laughter a-plenty in this wintery glow.
Our hearts beat in sync, a rhythm so bright,
In the harmony woven, we savor the night!

Notes from a Snowy Serenade

Under the stars, the snowflakes will dance,
I join in the fun, not missing a chance!
The air's filled with giggles, a snow-covered show,
As I try to impress with my frosty ballet flow.

But oops! There I go, with a slip and a spin,
A snowdrift's embrace is where I begin.
My friends gather 'round with their chuckles and grins,
This snowy serenade always ends with a win!

With carrots and buttons, we craft our own glee,
Our snowman's a sight, strangely happy as can be.
The stars twinkle softly, and not one snowflake's shy,
As they dance through the night, in the crisp, winter sky.

So let's raise our mugs to the fun and the cheer,
In winter's embrace, we've nothing to fear!
With laughter our soundtrack, we twirl in delight,
As the notes of this moment play through the night!

Serene Songs of Snowbound Nights

The winter's chill has come to play,
With frosty mischief all the way.
Snowflakes dance on fluffy ground,
Watch out for snowballs, flying round!

The cocoa's hot, the marshmallows float,
But I just spilled it on my coat!
With mittens warm, I grip my cup,
Oh, who knew snow could taste so up?

The snowman wobbles, with a crooked grin,
Each carrot-nose is stuck in sin.
We laugh till sides are aching sore,
As penguins sled from the neighbor's door!

At dusk we glide on our sleds of red,
Screams of joy, or was that dread?
As laughter echoes through the night,
We'll gear up for one more snowball fight!

Chilling Harmonies in the Cold

The wind's a joker, with icy breath,
It jokes about the frost and death.
Icicles hang like sharp-tongued fools,
While snow drifts pile like fluffy stools.

Frosty toes peek from beneath,
As we shuffle forward, oh my teeth!
The snowflakes giggle, twirl and spin,
While I trip over my own kin!

Hot soup spills on the snowy lane,
A secret blend of joy and pain.
With every slip and fall we find,
More ways to laugh, we're really blind!

So gather round, my pals so dear,
We'll toast our socks with a snowy cheer.
In this winter fun, we all agree,
Nothing beats laughter, not even a spree!

Tinkling Tunes Beneath the Stars

A winter night with stars so bright,
Under the moon, we start a fight.
With snowballs flying, laughter loud,
Our snowman's tip-top makes us proud!

The dogs are crazy, chasing tails,
While kids on sleds make silly trails.
The cocoa's thick, the cookies sweet,
Who knew winter could taste like a treat?

A snowman's hat that blew away,
Caused giggles and cheers throughout the fray.
With frozen fingers and rosy cheeks,
We dance around and play hide and tweaks!

In blankets thick, we'll cozy tight,
And share the tales of our snowy night.
For every fall is a badge we wear,
As memories dance in the frosty air!

Harmony of Crystal Laughter

The ground is white, the sky is gray,
But laughter spills in every way.
Snowflakes whisper silly tunes,
As we hide from the grumpy raccoons!

With every slip and icy glide,
Our laughter echoes far and wide.
The frosted branches sway along,
To the jolly rhythm of our song!

A snowball flies, and here it comes,
Right past my face, and then it hums.
A sneak attack, I'm on the floor,
The snowman now has my winter lore!

Under the stars, our giggles roam,
Turning this cold into a home.
For as long as snowflakes fall and spin,
We'll cherish laughter — let the fun begin!

Dances of Snowflakes in the Twilight

Frosty flakes twirl in delight,
They giggle and spin, oh what a sight!
Dancing high, they flap like birds,
While we sip cocoa and laugh at words.

A snowman wobbles with a carrot nose,
He jiggles and bounces, oh how he grows!
His button eyes wink, a cheeky smile,
As children slip and slide for a while.

Snowballs fly, a frosty fight,
Laughter echoes in the fading light.
Mom shouts, "Don't make too much mess!"
But kids just giggle, no need to stress.

The twilight dances, sparkles, glows,
As laughter bursts, and the cold wind blows.
In this winter mirth, we find our cheer,
With snowflakes laughing, winter's dear.

Whispers of Warmth in the Chill

The chill nips at fingers and toes,
But hot cocoa brings joy that flows.
Marshmallows float like fluffy boats,
As we gather 'round in our winter coats.

The fireplace crackles, the cats unwind,
While dogs dance around, they don't seem confined.
Throw a log, make the flames kiss the night,
Warmth in our hearts, what a wonderful sight!

The radio plays a quirky song,
As Uncle Joe sings—though he's off-key all along.
We laugh and tease, it's all in good fun,
As shadows flicker, our family's begun.

So here's to warmth in frosty air,
To funny moments that we all share.
With every sip, let the laughter swell,
In our cozy nook, all is well.

Frosted Secrets of Nightfall's Grace

Underneath the stars, snowflakes tell,
Whispers of secrets, all is well.
The moon peeks through with a giggle so bright,
While rodents sneaky, dance in the night.

The ice on the pond comes alive with glee,
As penguins in party hats slide with a plea.
"Join us!" they laugh, in tuxedos too,
While children gaze, and the sky turns blue.

Snowmen plot, as they gather around,
In their frosted coats, conspiratorial sound.
"What if we rolled down the hill as a team?"
With squeals of joy, it's the winter's dream!

The night deepens, embers glow fair,
In this funny realm, with frosty air.
So raise a toast to the sparkling scene,
Where laughter dances, happy and free!

Winter's Heartbeat in the Air

The snowflakes drop, a playful shower,
While snow-dogs prance, full of power.
The wind whispers jokes, but we can't hear,
As scarfs are tangled, bringing cheer!

Banana peels hide beneath the white,
And every slip makes giggles ignite.
A dad lands face-first in a snowy mound,
The kids erupt with laughter abound!

Frosty pine trees wear hats of frost,
Wobbling wreaths on doors, they exhaust!
We sip steaming treats, smiles so wide,
In this winter wonder, we take pride.

So here's to the fun that the cold brings near,
To snowy antics and hearty cheer.
With winter's pulse, we dance and sway,
In this frosty magic, we love to play.

The Frosted Parade of Dreams

Down the street they clatter loud,
Pigs in scarves, oh how they proud!
Chasing snowflakes on their tails,
While giggling folks, they share tall tales.

Laughter echoes, watch them slide,
Kittens tumble, full of pride.
Snowmen join the silly game,
One has lost his hat, oh what a shame!

A dog in boots takes a grand leap,
While crows above are counting sheep.
The world is frosted, full of cheer,
Who knew winter brings such fun near?

With twinkling lights and frothy drinks,
Elves dance wildly as the crowd winks.
In this parade of bright delight,
Let's laugh and play all through the night!

Jingle Trails Through Winter's Breath

Through the park, the snowflakes twirl,
Cats in hats give a playful whirl.
Hot cocoa spills with a splashy cheer,
While snowmen grin from ear to ear.

Giant mittens on a cat,
He pounces, bounces, simply fat.
A snowball fight goes out of hand,
As people slip and make a stand.

A rabbit hops with a carrot stick,
In boots too big—it's quite a trick!
As laughter rings from child to child,
Winter's charm is always wild.

With jingly tunes and dance galore,
The frosty air ignites the roar.
So let's embrace this snowy spree,
In jingle trails, we all agree!

Bell Tones Across the Snowy Vale

Amidst the drifts, with clinks and clacks,
Donkeys strut as they wear their packs.
Whistles echo through frosty air,
Bold penguins dive, oh what a flair!

Pigeons dressed in tiny coats,
Hockey skates for playful goats.
They glide and slide, all around,
As laughter rides upon the sound.

With each flurry, the giggles grow,
The magical charm of winter's show.
Come join the fun, it's quite the scene,
While nutty creatures hop between.

So trudge through drifts with joyful hearts,
As bonkers antics soon impart.
Under the moon's cold silver glare,
Let's laugh aloud, we haven't a care!

Celestial Cadence of the Season

As winter wraps the world in white,
Frogs in boots prepare for flight.
They leap and croak with merry songs,
While caroling along where they belong.

Chubby children roll the snow,
Impromptu parties start to grow.
Neighbors peek from windows wide,
Their laughter shared, no need to hide.

With snowball bombs and flurry fights,
Silly snowflakes create delights.
The figure skaters spin and twirl,
While excited pups begin to hurl.

A wink from winter's playful breeze,
Transforms the cold to purest glee.
So bundle up and join the fun,
For winter's dance has just begun!

Joyous Echoes Through the Pines

In winter's chill, we laugh and play,
With snowflakes dancing all the way.
We roll in drifts, a snowball fight,
Our cheeks are rosy, pure delight.

The forest echoes with our glee,
As we sled down hills, wild and free.
A chipmunk watches, cheeks stuffed tight,
He's nibbling nuts, a funny sight.

A snowman stands, his eyes askew,
With carrots misplaced, a funny view.
We giggle hard, his hat's too small,
This snowy day, we have a ball!

With voices loud, we sing our tune,
The frosty air, it makes us swoon.
In pines so tall, our joy takes flight,
In winter's land, everything feels right.

The Whispering Snowflakes' Song

A flurry falls, they whisper low,
Each flake a promise, soft and slow.
They tickle noses, melt on tongues,
In this brisk world, we feel so young.

A snowball flies, it hits the tree,
"Hey, watch it!" yells my friend with glee.
A snowman's hat is blown away,
He dons a bucket—hip, hooray!

Icicles dangle, sharp and bright,
We swing them low, like swords in flight.
"I'm a knight!" I shout, in chilly quest,
With winter's armor, we feel our best.

The snowflakes giggle, swirl around,
Our laughter echoes, all around.
In this white wonder, we belong,
As flakes dance lightly, to our song.

Crisp Harmonies Under the Stars

The stars above twinkle in glee,
While we sip cocoa by the tree.
"More marshmallows!" I yell with cheer,
Hot drinks and laughs are what we steer.

The fire crackles, shadows prance,
My friend insists he'll take a chance.
He jumps in snow, a comical flop,
And yells, "I'm Snowman! Don't you stop!"

The moonlight casts a silver glow,
Our silly antics steal the show.
A snow angel flaps in super style,
With outstretched wings, he claims his mile.

A burst of laughter fills the night,
As we embrace this pure delight.
With jolly hearts and silly dreams,
This winter night is bursting seams.

Luminous Dreams in Winter's Grasp

In winter's hold, we dance and glide,
With pockets full of joy and pride.
The icy path is our delight,
We twirl and spin, hearts feeling light.

Snowflakes tumble, soft and pale,
As we construct our fluffy trail.
"Oh no!" I shout, my hat is gone,
My head now cold, but I carry on!

We laugh out loud, a joyful sound,
While playful snowmen claim the ground.
With carrot noses, their hats all funny,
Our world of white feels bright and sunny!

With dreams aglow, we trek the nights,
In winter's realm, with starry sights.
Together we weave, a tapestry,
Of laughter, warmth, and purest glee.

Celestial Chatter Among the Snow

Tiny flakes fall, they spin and sway,
Hats and scarves in a grand ballet.
A snowman winks, or is it a tease?
As kids tumble down, aiming to please.

Snowy trails twist, a serpentine dance,
Elves lose their map, no need for a glance.
Laughter erupts, like fireworks in flight,
Muffin crumbs fly, oh what a sight!

Polar bears giggle, ducks sporting a grin,
Turtles in jackets, oh where to begin?
Frosty breath puffing, a cloud of delight,
Come join the frolic, winter's in sight!

Snowball fights start, the chaos ensues,
While penguins cheer, with their quirky views.
In this frosty realm, where laughter ignites,
We dance through the snow, under twinkling lights.

The Quiet Merriment of Winter

In the still of night, the moon starts to grin,
While socks play hide and seek with a pin.
Frosty gusts whistle, like a jolly old chap,
Wrapped in warm blankets, we fall for the nap.

Puddles reflect, a starry delight,
While mittens complain of the snowy bite.
A jolly old man, with a raucous cheer,
Makes cookies vanish, oh how they disappear!

Chased by a dog, through the thick fluffy quilt,
Around the snowman, their laughter is built.
Sliding on ice like a fish on a pier,
As winter's antics bring everyone near!

But oh! A tumble, who made that big splash?
The dog laughs harder, a wintertime clash.
Through giggles and warmth, we find our own cheer,
In this frosty adventure, with hugs sincere!

A Symphony of Snow and Stars

Each flake a note in a grand winter song,
As critters unite, where all of us belong.
Chipmunks in style, with hats far too bright,
Tap dance in rhythm, under soft moonlight.

Snow forts arise, a fortress of cheer,
As wild sled rides bring laughter near.
Celestial whispers wrap us up tight,
Making snow angels, oh what a sight!

The stars lean in, to hear all the fun,
As puppies chase tails, on the run.
With cocoa in hand, and smiles galore,
We're wrapped up in joy, who could ask for more?

The snowmen wear ties, what's that all about?
A winter soirée, with laughter and shout.
Frosty treble, and the bass denotes,
This season of glee, in whimsical coats!

Frosty Whispers of the Heart

Sugar plum fairies mingle with snow,
While rabbit-like whispers leave not a trace, so low.
A dance with the snowflakes, twirling in joy,
As snowmen tell secrets, oh what a ploy!

Icicles glimmer, they giggle and sing,
While squirrels and birds do their winter fling.
Hot cocoa rivers flow, marshmallows dive,
A tummy tickle, oh how we thrive!

With laughter like magic, and stories so bold,
Winter's own book, filled with tales to be told.
Pine trees don wigs, they're fabulous sights,
Chasing winter woes with pure, sweet delights.

So grab all your friends, let's make a parade,
With snowball confetti, and joyful charades.
Under laughter and stars, let this season pour,
The warmth of our hearts, forever to adore!

The Dance of Snowy Nights

Frosty flakes come tumbling down,
A jolly snowman wears a frown.
He lost his hat, it flew away,
Now he's cold and underplay.

Kids in boots run all around,
Chasing snowballs, laughter sounds.
One slipped hard, went for a ride,
Face first into the snow drift wide.

The dog hops up, joins in the fun,
Rolling 'round, he thinks he's won.
With every bounce and joyful bark,
He paints the white ground, leaving a mark.

As night falls, we gather tight,
With cocoa mugs, a cozy sight.
A snowman's nose, a carrot bright,
But even he can't get it right!

Celestial Chimes in the Chill

Dancing shadows, moonlit glow,
Carrot-nosed ducks begin to row.
They quack and flail, a silly lot,
Who knew they'd be such a hotshot?

Snowflakes twirl like ballerinas,
While penguins cheer like hyena's.
One tries to glide, slips on its beak,
Lands in a snowdrift, mud on its cheek.

The cat sneaks up, ready to pounce,
On a pile of snow, oh, what a bounce!
It hits the ground, a snowball flop,
Now it's all fluff, can't stop, can't stop!

A choir of owls hoot on cue,
While squirrels plan their great debut.
Snowmen giggle, their noses a mess,
In this chill party, we leave to impress!

A Frosty Waltz Unfolds

Under stars with chilly grace,
Snowmen dance, all over the place.
With twirls and spins, they lose their hats,
Now they look like clumsy cats!

Hot cocoa spills, a marshmallow fight,
Everyone's giggling, what a sight!
Fluffy clouds make their own parade,
While penguins practice their charade.

The air smells sweet, of peppermint dreams,
Chubby cheeks glow, or so it seems.
As mittens fly and laughter roars,
A parade of joy, in winter's scores.

The night rolls on, with frosty cheer,
While snowflakes fall, a fluffy veneer.
We'll cherish this dance, so fun and bright,
With whimsy wrapped in snowy white!

Sounds of Winter's Embrace

The shovels scrape with a squeaky sound,
As old men ramp up the snowy mound.
But one slips and does a dive,
A living snow angel, he feels alive!

Hotcakes sizzle, the maple flows,
Mom shouts loudly, just strike a pose!
But dad in snow pants looks like a blob,
Flailing around, what a funny job!

The cat leaps high, off the porch rail,
But a snow drift catches its tail!
Now it wiggles, a bundle of fluff,
Of winter antics, this is just enough.

With giggles shared in frosty air,
We rally 'round for snowy dare.
As merry hearts hold laughter dear,
The winter fun keeps drawing near!

Tinkling Tales from the Frozen Woods

In the woods where whispers play,
A rodent dons a hat of grey.
With tiny boots, he makes a dash,
Avoiding snowballs made in a flash.

A rabbit hops without a care,
While squirrels giggle in mid-air.
They build a fort, then take a stand,
With acorns flying, what a band!

A flurry comes, they ski with glee,
While icy slides shout, "Come and see!"
The frosty air is filled with cheer,
As woodland critters draw near.

So join the fun, with laughter loud,
In the snowy haven, be proud.
Remember the tales, both silly and bright,
Of nature's frolic, a pure delight!

The Pulse of an Icy Wonderland

In a land where snowflakes dance,
Frogs leap high, they take a chance.
Wearing scarves, so snug and neat,
Trying hard to keep the beat.

Chubby penguins slide on ice,
Wobbling 'round, looking quite nice.
With every slip, they crack a grin,
For waddle races, they sure win!

Frosted trees join in with cheer,
As moose prance by, oh so near.
They trumpet joy, but wait, oh no!
A snowman's hat launched in a blow!

Laughter rings in crisp blue skies,
As winter's charm, in jokes, lies.
With playful hearts and spirits bold,
These tinsel tales will never get old!

Jingle Journeys Through the Woods

Off we go on snowy trails,
Where giggles echo, tell the tales.
A bear tries snowball rolling vast,
But each one's tumbling, oh so fast!

The fox wears boots that squeak so loud,
As rabbits leap, happy and proud.
The frost crunches 'neath tiny paws,
Creating comic winter draws.

With candy canes, they race and twirl,
Around the trees, in a dizzy whirl.
When winter brings such funny sights,
All woodland friends embrace delights.

So grab a friend and swirl around,
In this frozen, joyous playground.
For laughter echoes through the night,
In our woodland party, pure delight!

Frosted Notes upon the Breeze

In frosty air, where spirits fly,
Snowflakes twirl, they kiss the sky.
A cat in mittens, chasing fluff,
With every bounce, things get tough!

Chipmunks in socks throw snowballs wide,
Trying their best to win the ride.
They tumble down a snowy hill,
Squeaking joy in a winter thrill.

A moody owl sings a tune,
While squirrels dance beneath the moon.
They flap and flap, with giddy grace,
Competing for the best snow face.

So join this frosty droll affair,
With icy giggles filling the air.
In winter's tale, with laughs to greet,
Remember, it's joy that makes us complete!

A Dance of Candy-Cane Colors

In the frosty air, they prance with flair,
Red and green stripes, swirling everywhere.
With giggles and leaps, they slip on the ice,
Chasing sweet treats, oh wouldn't that be nice!

A slip here, a trip there, giggles abound,
Frosty noses and laughter, what a silly sound!
Sugar plums bouncing, they fly through the sky,
Landing in puddles, oh me, oh my!

With marshmallow friends, they twirl round and round,
Each puff of fluff is a joy to be found.
Hot cocoa spills as they dance with delight,
Warming up cold hearts on this jolly night!

So grab your good friends, don't sit and pout,
Make merry mischief, dance 'til you shout!
Wrap yourself tight in colors so bright,
A fun candy-cane party awaits tonight!

Soundtrack of the Season's Chill

A whoosh and a waddle, a snowman's tap dance,
Chattering teeth join in for a chance.
With hats flying high, all the mittens take flight,
The cold gets a tune, it's a frosty delight!

Penguins play piano on ice like pros,
Tapping and flapping, as everyone knows.
Snowflakes take turns, like tiny musicians,
Playing in sync with their snow-covered visions.

Around frosty corners, the laughter does ring,
As frost-covered chums tune up to sing.
With hot cider sipped and cheeks rosy-red,
The chilly trombone plays on, it's said!

Watch out for the cat, in its snow-dusted coat,
It thinks it's a dog and it's trying to float.
With chimes and some laughter, and winter's sweet chill,
The soundtrack's a riot, it fits like a thrill!

Melodies from the Frostbitten Lane

On frosted paths where snowflakes twirl,
Penguins wear scarves, give a spin and a whirl.
With a tap-tap-tap, and a spin of the hat,
They waddle and jiggle, imagine that!

A snowball choir sings in the crisp, cold air,
While the postman mumbles, "I just don't care!"
He slips on a patch, oh, the sight is grand,
With letters and parcels plopping in hand.

The mailboxes giggle as they sway with glee,
While frost-covered critters join in on the spree.
Laughter erupts as the snowmen take aim,
A snowball fight breaks, oh, this whimsical game!

So dance through the lane, let your worries go,
With pitter and patter, we'll bask in the glow.
The melodies linger, all frosty and bright,
Creating a winter, silly-sweet night!

Twinkling Tidings on the Wind

The lanterns are giggling, they flicker and sway,
As snowflakes drop down in a glittery ballet.
With tinsel as capes, the trees bend with pride,
They know it's the season, and joy can't hide!

Carrots for noses, hats perched on top,
The snowmen are dancing, and they just won't stop.
With a strut and a jump, they sway all around,
Creating a ruckus, what mischief they've found!

Underneath twinkling lights, they hustle and glide,
Riding snowmobiles, what a comical ride!
Banana peels flying, the cat gives a yowl,
As they all race ahead, oh, what a howl!

With joy in their hearts and snow in their hair,
They prance through the night, without any care.
So join in the fun, with your warm-hearted kin,
Let laughter and light be the dance that you spin!

Winter's Whispered Harmonies

Flakes are swirling all around,
As my dog leaps with playful bound.
He slips and slides, a goofy dance,
While I just laugh at his lost chance.

Frosted trees in shimmering light,
We build a snowman, oh what a sight!
But when he tips, he takes a dive,
And that's how winter comes alive!

Hot cocoa spills, oh what a mess!
As marshmallows fly, I must confess.
We chase the snowballs, dodging glee,
But end up buried under a spree!

In this winter fun, we roam so free,
Chasing joy beneath each frosty tree.
The giggles echo, crisp and bright,
As laughter lingers into the night.

Echoes of Joy Beneath the Snow

The sledding hill, a laughter spree,
We race each other, who'll win—let's see!
With every bump, we giggle loud,
While landing flat, we form a crowd.

A cat in boots with no finesse,
Tries to conquer fun, but what a mess!
She tumbles thrice, then gives a stare,
As snowflakes settle in her hair.

Snowballs fly, oh! Watch that throw!
It backfired quick, a friend says, "No!"
We laugh till tears freeze on our cheeks,
In this chilly world, it's joy that speaks.

Winter magic fills the air,
With lights and warmth that we all share.
The echoes of joy ring out so clear,
As laughter dances, winter's cheer.

Crystal Clear Sounds of a Chilly Night

Under the moon, the world in white,
We hear the crunch, it feels just right.
With every step, a symphony,
Of winter's charm and silliness spree.

The frosty air, a canvas vast,
We shout out loud, our voices cast.
But then a snowball flies with flair,
"Nailed you!" I cheer, as snow flies everywhere!

Snowflakes twirl, a ballet bold,
As friends take a tumble, laughter unfolds.
We roll in the snow, like kids so spry,
While penguins dance and seagulls fly.

The world aglow in chilly glee,
With every laugh, a memory.
These crystal sounds of joy ignite,
Our hearts warmed up on this frosty night.

The Enchantment of Ice and Echoes

In frosty fields with joy we roam,
Chasing our shadows far from home.
But oh, my hat blows off again!
I run to catch it, what a win!

With icy pots and playful winds,
We skate like stars, like childhood friends.
But down I go, a slip, a slide,
And there I lie, with snow as my guide!

A winter's tale of giggles near,
The echoes of fun spread warmth and cheer.
And if we fall, we stand back tall,
For winter's laughter enchants us all.

So raise your voice, let laughter sing,
Under the moon, let joy take wing.
In this wonderland of playful tunes,
We'll dance 'til dawn beneath the moons.

Milton Keynes UK
Ingram Content Group UK Ltd.
UKHW031318271124
451618UK00007B/237